The Woman on the Shelf

by Lisa Jane McAuley

This book is dedicated to my niece, Grace.

'Though your beginning was small,

your latter end would increase abundantly.'

CONTENTS

INTRODUCTION

Up front, I just want to say sorry for the title of this book - and thank you for still purchasing it regardless.

I know what you must be thinking, "isn't 'The Woman on the Shelf' the worst title for a book aimed at single women?" Is that not what we hate being said about us, when people look sympathetically at us and then turn and whisper disparagingly to their friend, "Oh look at poor so and so, in her thirties, so pretty, and still 'on the shelf'. What a shame?"

Shame.

Singleness equals shame in many people's minds. But it is the shame of singleness that prompted me to write this book. In the society we live in today it seems that we ought not to be alone. It seems that being single looks like we are unloved, or at least waiting to be loved by that 'special someone,' which will then fulfil us and give us the license to get on with the rest of our lives.

The hopelessness and desperation that is associated with singleness is something that I want to address and dispel in this book. That is why I have called this book 'The Woman on The Shelf,' because by the time you have finished reading it I hope you see that being single or 'on the shelf' is not something to be despised, but a season in your life to be cherished and an opportunity to be seized.

So please, try and get over your offence and questions regarding the title of the book and hang in with me until the end. Hopefully it will make more sense by then.

First of all, let me tell you what led me to write this book.

Before I even thought about writing a book, any book, not just this book, I was struggling with my own state of singleness and having a moan to God about it and He said to me,

"If you feel like you're on the shelf, then fill that shelf with three things – worship, friendship and purpose."

I guess He was saying that I didn't have to be alone on the shelf.

- Worship is about my relationship with Him.
- Friendship is about my relationship with other people.
- Purpose is about what I can do with those relationships.

Suddenly the shelf didn't seem so lonely anymore.

I have learned a lot about these things; I have allowed Him to teach me how to worship Him in spirit and truth. I have met many people, some of whom became my closest friends, and others who haven't but I have still learned through that as well, and I have discovered quite a bit about purpose, of which this book is a part.

So this book is about my shelf and some of the lessons I have learned while being on my shelf and how I have come to realise it is not the worst place in the world and how I am still loved and accepted and of use and value while I am here.

He showed me truths about some single women in the Bible who didn't allow their singleness to deplete them in any way and I want to share these stories.

But the first story I want to share is my own....

My Story

One day I was praying and asking God for a husband. Ok, I know, this sounds a little desperate but I want to stress that I didn't get up every single morning and say, "God, please give me a husband. In Jesus' name. Amen." But there were times when I would sit down and have a conversation with God about my future and, like most women, I felt marriage was a significant part of that. We trust Him for the small everyday things but sometimes we need to talk to him about the big picture and what we think it will look like and what we want it to look like. From time to time I do this with God, it's like we exchange ideas. I tell Him what is on my heart for the years ahead and then He tells me what is on His heart. This was one of those conversations - big picture, long term, rest of my life, anyway, that is what I was doing. I was using the Scripture which is quoted at nearly every Christian wedding, "one shall put a thousand to flight and two shall put ten thousand to flight" (Deuteronomy 32:20 NIV). I was earnestly praying, "Lord, I want to increase my potential for You to use me. Give me someone so I can increase my power by ten-fold." It was all very heartfelt and earnest and I believed I was praying for very righteous, godly reasons, but suddenly God spoke back to me and said,

"Why would I trust you to put to flight ten thousand when you haven't even put to flight the one thousand I've already entrusted to you?"

Woah!!! Talk about a slap up the face!

Suddenly in that moment I got it. I saw that there was reason and purpose for my life as it was in that very moment. God could use me just as I was, single, lonely, broken, insecure, and unsure of my future - the list goes on and on. I still had one thousand to put to flight! I still had purpose to fulfil in this season of my life. Until now I thought I was in a waiting room. No one does anything in a waiting room. I hate waiting. I hate doctors' waiting rooms. I hate waiting in airports. There is no sense of purpose, people are just waiting for what's ahead, waiting to be called, but our life with God should not be like that. We have been chosen from before the foundation of the earth; He has good plans for us (Jer 29:11). We do not need to wait for God to call us. Why? Because He already has. In Jeremiah chapter 1 God tells Jeremiah that before he was born he was known and appointed by God. The same is true for us as it says in Eph 2:10, he prepares our "works beforehand that we should walk in them" (NKJV). There are obviously times when we need to wait on God but we do not need to wait for God to call us. But it took me a long time to realise this.

In my mind I had decided that by the age of thirty I would like to be at least in a relationship with the man I was going to marry, if not actually married to him. I wanted the security of knowing that part of my life was all sown up. So when I turned thirty and I was still single with no sight of any man appearing on the horizon, subconsciously I sat down, folded my arms and got in a very bad mood with God. Of course I had no idea I was doing it at the time, but in my heart I was saying, "That's it God, I'm doing nothing more for You until You get me a man!"

I had spent my twenties serving God full-on. My parents were pastors of a church and I was employed by that church. So I not only worked during the day at church but then came home to my parents and watched them go through the inevitable church hassles and heartbreaks (that's material for another book!). I was happy and honoured to be there for them and was very aware that this was my assignment for that time in my life. I was so glad that I had been single during that time as I was able to devote myself entirely to the work I was involved in and, to be honest, having someone else in my life then could have been complicated and messy.

Then my parents' ministry changed and they stepped down from pastoring and went into itinerant ministry. I left church employment and went into a new job in the community and voluntary sector. When I left the church we were in I said to God, "Thank You for this assignment You gave me. It's been an honour and a privilege to serve You, but there's just one thing I am asking, whatever my next assignment is, please don't let me have to do it alone. Please provide me with someone to serve alongside me." That was, and still is, my main reason for wanting to get married. My greatest desire is to find someone with whom I can share destiny.

I just want to serve God alongside someone. I want my dream and my husband's dream, even though they may be different, to complement each other and serve the eternal purposes of God.

Anyway, time passed and no-one came along, and I continued in my grudge against God.

However God has a way of moulding your heart to His purposes in such a beautiful manner that you can't help but say 'yes,' not out of coercion but with a willingness to honour the work He does in your life and to please Him simply because you love Him.

So the moulding process began, and it began simply and out of the blue. One afternoon I found myself sitting on my sofa with my Bible and being surrounded by loads of books. Suddenly, I heard His gentle whisper, "You're going to be a writer. You're going to write words that are going to set people free." Now, I had never written before. I wasn't even terribly good at English when I was at school, but in an amazing way, when God said that to me, it seemed the most natural thing for Him to say and it was the most natural thing for me to say, "Yes. Of course I am." So I began to write, and write, and write, and write...

Those first writings were not for anyone else. They were personal and for me. I realised that if my writing was ever going to set people free, it first had to set me free, and that is exactly what happened. As I wrote, words came tumbling out of me that scared me.

These are just a small portion of the words I wrote at the time:

- *This is the freedom journey. the freeing of my mind from negative thoughts which lead to negative actions. Thank you that you are bringing healing where it matters.*

I do not love myself as others love me which is how I have been living. Forgive me. No more. The order is: you love me - I love you - I love me - I love others. So simple but it really has to be in order for me to get it. Help me not just to see this truth but to live it.

• *This is my centre of gravity. What keeps me grounded. This is where I get true release. I know You love what I write here because it's just for You. Help me not to care about anyone else's opinion. Just Yours. You determine where this goes from here. Thank You for putting people in my life that keep me from the edge but at other times push me off it. I need both. Only as we fall do we discover our wings. And ultimately You are always there to catch us.*

• *Why should I apologise for who I am or how I am? Yet I feel like I go through life with a big question mark over my head, questions that people have asked and now questions that I'm asking. I'm tired of the questions. Yet I know they need to be asked, especially by me at the moment because it's how I break down the wall of silence around me. I've sat inside that prison for years inflicting damage on myself because I was too afraid to yell out. Too afraid to say how alone I felt, how ugly I felt, how weak I felt. Well that's it. I am done feeling ashamed. I am done being silent. I am done feeling inferior. I am done feeling insecure. I am done feeling unworthy of love, either from God or people. I am done feeling pitied. I am done putting other people in the place of Daddy. I am done banging my head off a brick wall. I am done having a broken heart. I am done being paranoid. I'm done trying. Would the real Lisa please stand up? Oh no, I can't, I'm in a wheelchair. That's my confession and I'm not ashamed.*

• *Freedom is not a destination but a journey. I am well and truly on that journey...*

It has made me remember it has made me forget.
It had made me laugh it has made me cry
It has made me say hello it has made me say goodbye
It has taken me forward, it has taken me back, it has taken me around
the world

It is a never ending journey
It is teaching me to love

Love myself just exactly as I am

I did not realise how messed up I was until I started intensely pounding on the keyboard. I also never knew truth until I started uncovering all those layers. In the process, the truth I was starting to know was indeed setting me free. God was moulding me into the person He created me to be.

Along with that freedom came an awareness of a responsibility. God didn't set me free just so I could feel good. He had a plan and a purpose for that freedom. So the challenge came, "What are you going to do with the freedom you have attained?" I started writing a blog and thought that was enough, I thought that was me doing my bit, but God wanted more - He always wants more. I was still thinking about my singleness and was very reluctant to step out and write more because of what I had earlier said to God, "Don't let me do this next assignment alone." That's when He hit me up the face with the verse in Deuteronomy. There was still a purpose for my being single. I hadn't put to flight all my one thousand. I had maybe killed off seven hundred or 650 or 986 or 999 but there were still some I had to finish off.

In Psalm 139:16 it says: "in Your book they were written. The days fashioned for me when as yet there were none of them" (NKJV). He asked me directly, "Do you trust Me to be the author of your life? I have already written your book. The heavenly copy is finished. Do you trust Me to write the chapters in the right order? You want the romance chapter to happen now but I have another destiny chapter for you to write. Will you write it? Are you willing to take on one more assignment while you are still single?" I'll be honest and say that I struggled answering that and I didn't answer straight away. But eventually I said yes and that 'yes' is what you are holding in your hand right now.

Ruth's Story

Ecclesiastes 1:9 says, "There is nothing new under the sun!" (NKJV). I am not the first person to write about singleness. The structure for my book has been in front of me all along! It is found in the book of Ruth. It was this book that really spoke to me about my singleness and gave me hope in this season of my life.

In July 2009 I went to Brazil with my parents to visit my brother who lived there at the time. He lived in the north of the country but in the middle of the holiday we took a trip to visit Rio de Janeiro. Before we left for the holiday and I found out we were going to Rio there was just one place I was so excited to go and see. That place was the statue of Christ the Redeemer. For weeks and weeks beforehand God had been showing me so much truth from His Word about redemption and that truth was setting me free from so many lies that had held me captive all my life. Then I realised I was going to see the statue called Christ the Redeemer; not Christ the Saviour or Christ the Healer but Christ the Redeemer. I just knew that if God was taking me across the world to see this then there was a very clear message He wanted to communicate to me. God speaks to you through His Word, most importantly, but we are three-part beings, spirit, soul and body (1 Thess 5:23) and sometimes He has to speak to us in the realm of the physical in order to confirm what He is saying in the spiritual.

I was not wrong.

As I sat at the foot of the statue of Christ the Redeemer in Rio de Janeiro God spoke to me and said, "Just as Ruth found love in the arms of her redeemer, so you will find love in My arms." For the rest of that holiday I bathed in the pages of the book of Ruth. I found healing for my soul and hope for my future. It is Ruth's example that I follow as I see her worship, friendship and purpose all unfold in the few short chapters of her book in the Bible.

"Whose young woman is this?" (Ruth 2:5 NKJV). This was the question asked by Boaz as he observed Ruth gathering the leftovers after the harvesters in his field. There were many workers in that field, between paid harvesters and the gleaners who followed behind. Obviously she stood out to him. She was different from the rest of the other workers in that field for him to have noticed her and asked such a question. What made her different? I believe it's because she handled her situation, her singleness, in a godly way. As I studied the life of Ruth I saw a pattern that God wanted me to follow.

After the death of her husband, Ruth found herself, very much, on the shelf. Naomi said to Ruth and her sister-in-law, Orpah before they left Moab, "Return home, my daughters. Why would you come with me? Am I going to have any more sons who could become your husbands? Return home, my daughters; I am too old to have another husband. Even if I thought there was still hope for me, even if I had a husband tonight and then gave birth to sons - would you wait until they grew up? Would you remain unmarried for them? No, my daughters." (Ruth 1:11-13 NIV).

Firstly, she cleared her shelf of all the negative stuff that was on it. She left behind her pain and grief. She cleared it of all hopes for a normal married life in Moab.

When she cleared her shelf of the negative, she filled it with the positive.

- Ruth's worship – 'your God shall be my God.' She placed worship on her shelf by declaring to Naomi, "Your God shall be my God (Ruth 1:16)." Ruth embraced the true God of Israel and left behind the idols of Moab.

- Ruth's friendship – 'entreat me not to leave you.' She placed friendship on her shelf when she "clung to Naomi" and cried out, "entreat me not to leave you" (Ruth 1:16). She chose the right person to do life with. She could have gone back to Moab with Orpah but she obviously saw qualities in Naomi that she wanted.

- Ruth's purpose – 'let me go to the field' She placed purpose on her shelf when she said, "let me go to the field" (Ruth 2:1), so that she could serve Naomi and provide food for them both. She could have sat in Bethlehem and felt sorry or have sat waiting for life to happen to her. She could have felt so unworthy to go out into the field as she was a despised foreigner, but she did not let any of that hold her back, nor did she waste this season. She arose and began to make a difference.

Do you see the pattern? I believe that this is the pattern God wants us, as single women, to follow.

- He wants us to place worship on our shelf, to put Him first. He wants us to learn to worship Him in spirit and truth.
- He wants us to put friendship on our shelf, to connect with the right people who will nourish our souls.
- He wants us to put purpose on our shelf, to use this season to serve others.

PART 1

Clearing the Shelf

God wants to fill our shelf with three things, worship, friendship and purpose, but sometimes our shelf can be a little crowded. So before God can put anything positive there He needs to remove some stuff that has been crowding our shelf and will get in the way of anything good He wants to place on it.

During the clearing of the shelf there is a time of emptiness when there is nothing there. You just have this blank, bare shelf and that is hard to handle. That is the time we want to give up and fill our shelf with anything just because its something to have on our shelf. We end up putting idols on our shelf. Idols of money, career or wrong relationships, but idols will never satisfy us. We fill our lives with empty pursuits just because it is something to do.

Before we can attract anything or anyone into our lives our first priority must be attracting God into our lives. He is the foundation on which we build everything else. The good news for us is that God is attracted to emptiness and brokenness. In Genesis 1:2 it says that the earth was "without form and void" (NKJV). The literal meaning of "without form" is formlessness, confusion, unreality, emptiness. It also means a place of wilderness, a solitary place. Sound familiar? Do you ever feel like your life has no order and is just completely empty? You just seem to drift from day to day not seeing any clear purpose? You don't feel like you are living the life you were destined to live - you are just existing. I cannot tell you how many times I have felt that way.

But there is hope. In the very next sentence it says: "the Spirit of God was moving (hovering, brooding) over the face of the waters. Then God said, 'Let there be light.' And there was light" (Gen 1:2-3 AMP). We belong to a God who can create something from nothing, but, most of the time, He is waiting for us to empty ourselves of all that we have in order to do something incredible in our lives. It is our 'stuff' that hinders him. We don't just see this happen at creation. There are several instances in the Bible where God demands emptiness and brokenness in order to fulfil His purpose.

There is a story in 2 Kings 4 where a widow was in dire financial straits and she went to the prophet Elisha to ask for help. He says to her, "Go, borrow vessels from everywhere, from all your neighbours, empty vessels; do not gather just a few" (2 Kings 4:3 NKJV). Note that he says *empty* vessels. Had there not been emptiness, the miracle could not have taken place. As the widow began to pour the oil into the vessels, it was as if the emptiness in the vessels kept encouraging the oil to keep on pouring. It was only as the emptiness finished that the oil finished. She asked her son to bring her another vessel and he replied, "'There is not another vessel.' So the oil ceased" (2 Kings 4:6 NKJV). Emptiness attracts God's supply into our lives. If you are feeling empty right now, perhaps you are closer to your miracle than you think.

There is another incident in scripture where God uses empty vessels in a miraculous way. This is found in Judges 7 when Gideon and his armies are in battle against the Midianites. God tells Gideon to give each of his soldiers an empty vessel and a torch to put inside it. At the allotted time Gideon directs the army to break the vessels and let the torches shine. When this happened the enemy fled in confusion and the battle was won. The requirement for victory was that the vessels were empty and broken.

The Christian church today preaches a message of fullness and wholeness. So much so that we have lost the value of brokenness and what it means to God. He is not repelled by your broken life. He is attracted to it. In most cases it is the only thing necessary to fulfil His plan.

Mary of Bethany understood this. She had a very expensive vessel containing some very expensive perfume. It was whole and full, but in the eyes of her Saviour that wasn't good enough. It was only as the vessel was broken and the contents emptied over his feet that sense was made. Jesus said, "She has poured this perfume on me to prepare my body for burial" (Matt 26:13 NLT). That night, brokenness and emptiness served Jesus much more than wholeness and fullness. This vessel wasn't just opened, it was smashed. This was likely her only financial security, it could have been her dowry, the only thing she could have offered a prospective husband. It was the one possession that was her security. But she poured it all out on her Saviour. She let go of her security in adoration of Jesus. Can you do that?

The Bible calls us vessels of honour (2 Tim 2:21) chosen by God to fulfil His purposes on the earth. We are described as having "treasure in earthen vessels that the power may be of God and not of us" (2 Cor 4:7 NKJV). In this season are we willing to be empty and broken before Him so He can fill us with Himself? Can we stand the emptiness until He becomes our fullness? One of the names of God is Jehovah Shalom. Shalom literally means 'nothing missing, nothing broken.' As He is attracted to our emptiness and brokenness He fills it with His fullness and wholeness.

However, letting go is a painful process, but God cannot work until we do.

In Exodus chapter 4 we see that Moses, a mighty man of God, was forced to let go of something before God could use him. When he had that encounter with God at the burning bush, God asked him a question: "What is that in your hand?" (Ex 4:2 NKJV). Moses replied, "a rod." It was just a simple, boring, everyday piece of equipment. It was a shepherd's rod so it represented Moses' identity and security - just a shepherd. He had once been a prince of Egypt but because he messed up in the past he had to find a new identity and this was it, a mere shepherd, but God asked him to throw it on the ground. The one thing that he found refuge in. The one thing that brought him significance and security, God was asking him to throw it down. Surely it would do no good lying on the ground anyway. It would be much better to hold on to it.

Despite this Moses found somewhere within himself, the ability to let go. That staff was his support. Marriage is something that we look to as something we can lean on. We want someone else in our lives to support us in all we do. But can we let go of this dream even for a season? When our hands are empty that's when God can go to work. When Moses let go, God went to work. God took that insignificant piece of wood and did something miraculous. After Moses let go, God allowed that piece of wood to be the means of parting the Red Sea.

Only after you let go can God do something truly miraculous. He doesn't want to tear it from you. He wants you to lay it down in surrender, not knowing what may become of it. Today He is asking you, "what is that in your hand?"

Letting go

my hands are empty
holding nothing
ready to receive

love

purpose

destiny.

The D Word

This is the one word we, as single people, hate being thrown at us. I can hear it ringing in my ears now,

"Ooohh, she's in her 30s and she hasn't got a boyfriend, she must be desperate."

"She hasn't had a boyfriend for ages, she must be desperate."

"Ooooh, she's not married yet, she must be desperate."

And of course we just shrug it off and say that we are not bothered and we are totally relaxed about the whole thing because we believe in God's timing, and we have not met the right person yet, and it is totally fine and blah blah blah....

Can we be honest here in the pages of this book? I know I have been asked all these questions and I have given all these answers but deep down when I was being honest with myself, the "d word" was the perfect description for how I was feeling. I desperately wanted someone. I desperately wanted that companionship and I desperately wanted the security of knowing that part of my life was sorted out.

The definition of desperate is: "having an urgent need, desire; leaving little or no hope. Actuated by a feeling of hopelessness. Having no hope, giving into despair, leaving little or no hope."

I guess that definition is pretty accurate for how I felt at times, having "little or no hope." In Proverbs it says, "Hope deferred makes the heart sick" (Prov 13:12 NKJV). The word deferred here means, "to draw out, prolong, continue." There are many women walking around with sick hearts because of the hope that they are continually being denied. It feels like time and opportunity has passed them by and that lack of hope is slowly killing them. It feels like all that deferred hope has made them so sick that they are dying. Hope is like fuel to our souls. Look at it like this: you're driving along nicely then the car starts to cough and splutter and you realise you're not driving as fast as you once were. That's when you realise you're out of fuel - you can only drive so far on an empty fuel tank, then you stop. It is exactly the same when you run out of hope. You begin to slow down and then you eventually stop. This is where I have seen a lot of women settle for second best. But can I say something here?

When you have nobody, in your search for somebody, don't settle for just anybody.

You are better than 'just anybody.' God has someone so special for you that you cannot give into despair at the last minute and end up with someone who won't treat you like the amazing woman you are.

 Read these verses and let hope flood your soul:

Romans 15:13: "Now may the God of hope fill you with all joy and peace in believing, that you may abound in hope by power of the Holy Spirit" (NKJV).

Hebrews 6:19: "This hope we have as an anchor for the soul, both sure and steadfast" (NKJV).

Hebrews 11:1: "Now faith is the substance of things hoped for, the evidence of things not seen" (NKJV).

These are not my words, these are the words of God who loves and cares for you and has seen every tear you have cried and every anxious thought that has wandered through your mind. Romans 8:15 says that now we can cry out and address God as "Abba Father." This word, 'abba' is the word that Jewish children use to address their fathers. It is equivalent to our word 'daddy'. This is how God wants to be seen by us. Not as some austere, removed figure but as our Daddy. Picture yourself running into His arms being secure of his love.

In the midst of your desperation there is hope. Don't be ashamed to say it, "I am desperate." But don't forget to appendix it with, "but I belong to a God of hope and He will not see me abandoned. He will satisfy my need."

Reasons and Seasons

The devil is a liar!

Let that sink in.

He will tell you that it's too late and that you've missed your chance.

That is a lie from the pit of hell!!

It's a lie that I swallowed for quite some time. I thought my time had passed. I was nearly 30 and I wasn't in a relationship and there wasn't a prospect of one on the horizon – not with the men I knew at that time!! All I could hear was a big ticking clock and the time was running out, then God spoke to me and reminded me of the life that I had lived up till then. He reminded me about how I had set my mind to serve Him and had done so single-mindedly for years. He asked me, "Do you think I would deny you your greatest desire or keep you so busy that you would never attain it? If your heart has been for Me all this time and you have put Me first in all things. Then the reason you are not married yet is not because its too late, it simply hasn't been the right time until now." Then I realised that there are reasons and seasons for everything in life. If we can understand that with regard to singleness I believe we will be less frustrated and fearful about the whole thing.

In Ecclesiastes 3:1 it says, "To everything there is a season, A time for every purpose under Heaven" (NKJV).

Once I realised that singleness was just a season the pressure was off. There were no more regrets. No more looking over my shoulder wondering if I should have taken that road or this road. I knew my times were in His hands (Psa 31:15) and He had everything under control. It wasn't too late!!!! Phew!! I could take a deep breath and enjoy the season I was in because I was exactly where He wanted me to be at that time.

I always had a fear that I would never get married. You know how you hear of some women who are called to a 'life of singleness.' They were always really godly women who spent hours in prayer every day and were so holy it was unbelievable. Now, just ask anyone who knows me, I ain't really like that! But it was always my worst nightmare, "What if God calls me to that life? What if I spend my days wanting to be with someone but never getting the chance because God wants me to be single? What if I spend the rest of my life being miserable?" These are the kind of questions that floated round my head on a regular basis.

Then I realised that God loved me. That might seem like quite elementary thing but it took me years to get it, but once I did, it changed everything. If He loved me He wouldn't sentence me to a life of torture, making me do the thing I least wanted to do. His Word says that He gives us the desires of our hearts and I believe that if these desires are in accordance with His Word then we have nothing to worry about (Psa 37:4). If He did want me to be single for the rest of my life then I believe he would take the desire for marriage away from me and make me be 100% happy with being on my own. So far He hasn't done that so I'm happy to be in this season, but I did have to embrace this season.

At one point God brought me up close and personal with the thought of being on my own forever and it terrified me. What I was saying essentially to God was, "You're enough for me now but not in thirty years time." We have no control over how long these seasons last. We must learn to trust this season and that God has everything under control and He will bring us through this season at the right time. We cannot give in to the fear the enemy wants to plant in our hearts.

So we've established that there is a season, but a season for what? In Ecc 3:1 it says that there is a "time for every purpose under Heaven" (KJV).

Your season will not make any sense without knowing the reason for it - look for that reason. It is there. Don't let the devil bluff you into thinking this is a useless time in your life.

The reason is all around you, it is in the people you meet, the places you go. Only until now you have been so convinced that you weren't supposed to be doing anything that you haven't seen the reason. Once you realise God has created you to live in the here and now you look at people with new eyes and a new heart and you will stumble across opportunities to help them and, thus, fulfil your reason for this season.

Sinking or Synching?

I have to be honest and say that this next part has been the hardest part of the book to write. As soon as I began to write it, it was like I came up against a brick wall. For months I was unable to articulate anything of what needed to be said, then to cap it all off I had a fall and dislocated my elbow which meant I was physically unable to write anything at all!!

Why was it such a battle??

I feel it is because this is the most important part of the book. If you fail to understand and put into practice the principles laid out in the next few pages you may as well put the book down now and stop reading altogether. The worship, friendship and purpose God has in store for you all hinges on your ability to synchronise your thinking with His Word.

- Without it you will be unable to get a true revelation of God and His love and thus be unable to truly worship Him.
- You will have a negative image of yourself and feel unworthy of the friendship He wants to pour into your life.
- Because we see the world as we see ourselves we will then be unable to see beyond our own problems and so we will never fulfil the purpose He has placed on our lives in order to make a difference on this planet.

So you have read until now and perhaps you are beginning to hope that there is some reason for this season in your life. Perhaps you are realising that God has His perfect timing and you should not rush ahead of Him. You understand a higher purpose for all that is going on, or not going on, whatever the case may be, but even though you know all that, you still really want to be married.

Believe me I get that. Even in the writing of this book I have had to deal with these longings and not be controlled by them. There are times when I had to shut the computer down and walk away because it felt like it was just too hard. I knew God called me to write this, it was my purpose for this season but when God called me He didn't magically remove the desire from me. If anything, it intensified. It seemed like everyone around me was either getting married or engaged. I attended three weddings in the space of three months. One of my best friends got engaged and my sister also got engaged. So while I'm writing this book on singleness I am helping my sister plan her wedding and I will be her chief bridesmaid!! Now please understand, I am not resentful in any way, all of these marriages and engagements are answers to prayer and reasons for celebration, I could not be happier for everyone involved (you wanna see me at a wedding – I am first on and last off the dance floor!).

But there were times when I wished it was me....

It would have been very easy to look at everything going on around me and sink into feelings of hopelessness and despair, even bitterness.

It can be so easy to sink.

Peter did it. In Matthew 14, Jesus sent his disciples across the sea, yet although they were on that sea because Jesus sent them, it didn't mean that the journey was going to be a smooth one. It wasn't long before the wind started to howl and the waves came crashing into the boat. Then they saw Jesus. Even that did not calm the storm. Peter was brave and decided to step out and walk on the water. The waves still crashed, the wind still roared. You see what I mean here? If you are right in the centre of the will of God and stepping out to do amazing things for Him, you would think

He would make it easy for you, right? Wrong! If anything, it gets harder. Why? So that the truth of what you are accomplishing is so obviously coming from God that it cannot be denied.

When I committed to write this book I told God that I wanted the truth to come from the inside out. In other words, I didn't want to write something that I hadn't been living. I know that has meant that writing this book has become a longer process because of this commitment. Someone once told me, "You will never write better than you live." I don't just want to write well, I want to live well, because people are reading me everyday. So when it came to writing this section on managing your emotions and not sinking in despair, I had a lot of living to do before I could write one word. You see, this is where I sink. I look at what is going on around me and how that makes me feel and then before I know it I'm splashing about in the water gasping for breath.

But God is faithful and like He did with Peter, He has reached out His hand and pulled me up out of the water (Matt 14:31), and while I am no expert I can definitely share from experience that it is possible to not be controlled by those negative emotions that seem to overwhelm you.

So just how do you do that?

By synching instead of sinking....

The definition of synchronise is "to cause to go on, move, operate, work at the same rate and exactly together." What we need to do with our thoughts and emotions is to synchronise them to the Word of God and to what He says about our lives and situations.

I own a smartphone which has an operating system which allows it to work. From time to time the manufacturers will bring out a new operating system. Every time a new operating system is released I have to ensure my phone is synchronised with the new operating system.

Before we embarked on our relationship with God it's like our minds operated on our own operating system. But God operates on a different system so when we live our lives in accordance with His

Word we must synchronise our minds and emotions with the heavenly operating system.

Why is it so important to get our minds in sync? Because it says in Proverbs 23:7: "As he thinks in his heart, so is he" (NKJV). Basically this means you are what you think you are. So if you have convinced yourself that you are worthless and no good, then that is what you are and no one can convince you otherwise. If you have convinced yourself that you are incomplete without having that 'special someone,' then you will be. It is that simple.

There is a story in the Bible that really bears this out. It is the time when Moses sent out spies to view the promised land. Twelve spies were sent out in total, yet only two, Joshua and Caleb, returned with a good report. It is interesting to hear what the other ten said to Moses on their return. They said: "We were as grasshoppers in our own sight, and so we were in their eyes" (Num 13:33 NKJV). Notice – they were grasshoppers 'in their own sight' before they were grasshoppers in the giants' sight. Their view of themselves defined their enemy's view of who they were. Their enemy did not define them – they defined themselves because that's what they really thought about themselves.

How do you see yourself? Do you let your opinions of yourself and your emotions define who you are and what you can do? If so then you need to synchronise with the new operating system.

How do you do this?

In Romans 12:2 it says, "Be transformed by the renewing of your mind" (NKJV). Basically that means changing the way you think and what you think about. In the Psalms, David cried out, "Let the words of my mouth and the meditation of my heart be acceptable in your sight" (Psa 19:14). Are your thoughts acceptable to God? That's quite a vague question, I know, but we have to ask it as the first step to renewing our minds.

I have used the example of synchronising my smartphone in order to obtain the new operating system. When I do this it usually takes ten to fifteen minutes. Oh how I wish synchronising my mind with the heavenly operating system only took that length of time. Trust me, when you commit to renewing your mind, you are committing to a life-long process. Do not be discouraged by this. Everyday I have to bring my mind into check with the Word of God and not be ruled by my emotions. As a single woman in my mid-thirties, with what seems like everyone around me getting married I battle with loneliness, discontentment, resentment, fear and hopelessness. It is then that I have to "take every thought captive and bring it into subjection with the word of God" (2 Cor 10:5 NKJV). In my loneliness I have to declare that "He is the strength of my heart and my portion forever" (Psa 73:26 NKJV). In my resentment I have had to declare that I am "highly favoured" (Luke 1:28 NKJV). In my fear I have had to declare that His "perfect love casts out fear" (1 John 4:18 NKJV).

Do you see what I mean?

Did this change how I felt? Not immediately. But the Word says "you shall know the truth and the truth shall make you free" (John 8:32 NKJV). It doesn't say, "you shall feel the truth." That is where we make our mistake. We think that our feelings will change immediately after we begin this process but in most cases it is a process of being obedient and living by "faith and not by sight" (2 Cor 5:7 NKJV).

A key to being successful is realising that you have the authority to do this. You are made in the image of God, and as He is a three-part being so are we. We are a spirit, we have a soul (our mind, will and emotions) and we live in a body. When we became Christians our spirits were born again. This is the part of us which now commands our soul and body. You have to realise that your emotions are now subject to your spirit so eventually they must obey. Romans 8:5 says, "...but those who are controlled by the Holy Spirit think about things that please the Spirit" (NLT). We need to change what we think about.

I have had to do this. My greatest strength is also my greatest weakness - my imagination. As a writer and creative person I have the ability to imagine words on a page, the progression of a story, I can see a concept from beginning through to the end. It is a wonderful gift and I know it has been given to me from God. But there are times when that same gift has taken me down some paths that have caused me pain and left me feeling bereft.

My ability to daydream is extraordinary. I could spend hours imagining scenarios that are anything but godly. I can't tell you the amount of hours I have wasted imagining my prince charming coming to rescue me. I have become fixated and emotionally attached to people in my world and imagined being in a relationship with them. I have fallen in love purely through my imagination. This has left me heartbroken and almost crippled me emotionally as I was walking down a one way street. I was the one with all the love, getting nothing in return. I have had to learn over a long period of time to "bring every thought into captivity into the obedience of Christ" (2 Cor 10:5 NKJV). This took time as you cannot change overnight something that you have done for years. I am being very honest here as this has been such a big battle for me and one that I have fought very privately but I do not think I am the only one fighting this battle. We live in a world were everyone is looking for love. Some are lucky enough to find it with the right person at the right time but others fall in love with the wrong person at the wrong time. You may be struggling with the same thing. Perhaps it is a friend or an old boyfriend, and up until now you have been convincing yourself that your feelings are just platonic but deep down you know there is more. You know that there is part of you that cannot let go.

What do you do then?? Is there a way out??

Yes!!

Christ has come to set us free. He purchased freedom for us on the Cross. His death brought us healing – not just physical healing but emotional healing. His mind was tormented so that our minds don't have to be. I have been able to make this journey into freedom so I want to share some of the steps I had to take.

Firstly I had to acknowledge the truth, I had to acknowledge to myself and to God how I really felt. I could have lived in denial because that way I would never have had to face all the upcoming hurdles. I wouldn't have had to change. But then I feel my life would have come to a standstill and God would have been unable to make full use of the potential that was within me. It was a chokehold on my purpose, but once I acknowledged my weakness, the process of healing could begin.

The next step was to ask why? This was a recurring pattern in my life. From as young as I could remember I always fixated on someone. The issue really wasn't the person – it could have been anyone - but why did this always happen?. As I began to seek God and get to the root of the problem, He was so gracious and patient. God began to show me that it was because I had a distorted view of Him. All along, it was His love I craved for but because of wrong thoughts of Him and myself I looked in the wrong places so I settled for second best.

Once I understood the cause of the problem I could look for the remedy. In my case I needed a true revelation of the love of God. With all my heart and soul I began to seek this. Through the Bible, through books, sermons and music I began to fill my mind with His love. I surrounded myself with this truth and slowly my mind began to be renewed. Psalm 48:9 says, "we meditate in your unfailing love" (NLT). That is what I had to do. I had to force my mind to dwell on the love of God. Every time it wandered elsewhere I had to bring it back. Philippians 4:8 says, "Finally, brethren, whatever things are true, whatever things are noble, whatever things are just, whatever things are pure, whatever things are lovely, whatever things are of good report, if there is any virtue and if there is anything praiseworthy - meditate on these things" (NKJV). Meditate means to think about over and over, to ponder. For weeks and months I continually pondered the love of God then slowly the truth of that love began to penetrate the wall of lies that had surrounded my mind. It didn't come crashing down in one fell swoop but brick by brick it began to crumble. Light began to pierce through the darkness and the darkness couldn't overcome it (John 1:5 NKJV).

The next thing I had to change was my behaviour. I had to break contact with the person in question. Sometimes this was easy, as circumstances changed, but other times these people were part of my world and unavoidable so I needed to change the way I related to them. Close friendships had to be distanced and I needed to establish healthy friendships. This meant I had to make myself accountable to someone and it meant I had to be honest about how I felt and acted. This was hard as I felt so ashamed but I knew that this was the last hurdle in becoming whole. In the book of James it tells us to confess our sins to one another that we may be healed. Note that it doesn't say that we may be 'forgiven,' only God can do that, it says, "confess your sins and pray for one another that you may be healed" (James 5:16 NIV). True healing comes with true confession. I can't stress enough how much accountability will save you.

Once I took the mask off and confessed my weakness, hurt and pain I knew that true healing could take place. I was not hiding any longer. I gave my accountability partner the authority to keep a close eye on me and correct me if they saw my behaviour was not as it should be. This has been the biggest help to me and the thing that has made me stay on the path to true freedom.

I really have opened my heart to you in these last few pages but someone once said that your biggest pain can become your biggest platform. This has definitely been the biggest pain in my life – loving someone from afar and feeling the rejection, shame and loss it can bring but I hope that by sharing it with you it not only brings me freedom but brings you freedom also.

Please don't be ashamed of how you feel. You are on a journey to freedom, but this journey is taken one step at a time. Let God in. Let Him heal your heart. Allow yourself to be loved in the way you deserve to be loved.

PART 2

Placing Worship on the Shelf

"Your God Will Be My God" (Ruth 1:16)

Father, You have been my God since I prayed, at the age of six, a simple prayer and asked You to forgive me of my sin and come and live in my heart. I would be nowhere without You. Throughout all of my life You have never let go of my hand. May You always find my hands and my heart raised in worship to You.

Loneliness

The biggest issue I want to address regarding singleness is that of loneliness, probably because it's the biggest issue I have struggled with and, if I am honest, still struggle with. But God has spoken to me so much through my seasons of loneliness and has revealed so much of his love and grace I can truly say that's where I've found Him at the deepest level.

I have also encountered so much loneliness in the world around me, even in the family of God, that I want to dispel a few myths regarding it.

Firstly, Satan will make you feel that you are the only person who is lonely. He will make you feel that everyone else around you is in the perfect friendship or relationship and that you are the only person who has no one. That is a lie!! I was under that illusion for years and it kept me silent because I was ashamed. Ashamed to admit that I was lonely, somehow lacking. However, as soon as I began to be honest and talk about how lonely I was feeling, I was overwhelmed by the number of people who said that was how they also felt. I was surprised because it was people around me who I had perceived to be 'popular people.' Every time I saw them they were surrounded and were really involved in various activities but when they took the mask off they revealed how isolated they felt. Sure, they knew loads of people but they felt that they never really connected with anyone.

So why are people so afraid to admit to being lonely??? The reason I struggled with coming clean was because I thought that by admitting that I was lonely I was somehow saying that God wasn't enough for me, that my relationship with Him wasn't strong enough, that I didn't love Him enough and that His love wasn't enough for me. So that's why I stayed silent. I refused to bring this issue into the light and consequently I withered in the dark. Shame and fear clouded over me and kept me hidden, and thus kept my pain hidden. But Isaiah 54:4 says, "Do not fear for you will not be ashamed; neither be disgraced for you will not be put to shame; for you will forget the shame of your youth and not remember the reproach of your widowhood anymore." This is God speaking to a single woman in the Bible and telling her she doesn't have to be afraid or ashamed any longer. Once we remove the shame of loneliness then we can bring it into the light.

I am lonely, and I am not ashamed to say it anymore. One of the reasons I am not ashamed to say it is because I am not the first person to say it.

God is!

God is not enough for you!!

Let me take you back to the Garden of Eden. The first Person to mention loneliness in the Bible isn't Adam, it isn't Eve, it isn't the devil, it is God Himself. He said, "It is not good for the man to be alone" (Gen 2:18 NKJV). Now you have to be aware of when He said this. It wasn't after the fall when the whole world was in chaos. It was before sin entered the world and when God came down and walked in the garden with Adam "in the cool of the day" (Gen 3:8 NKJV). This is when they hung out and spent time together.

What must that have been like? What did they talk about? What did they do? It must have been incredible.

Even in the midst of all that perfection, God Himself said, "it is not good for man to be alone" (Gen 2:18 NKJV). Basically God was saying that He wasn't enough. Adam didn't say it, God did. That is why we should not be ashamed of feeling lonely because God created us to feel that way so that we would reach out and connect with the people around us. God intended us to have human connection as well as divine connection. That is why He made Eve for Adam. In the New Testament Paul writes about how we are part of a body and dependant on one another (Rom 12:5). If I hurt, you hurt; and if you hurt, I hurt. There's no getting away from each other. That is why being alone is so unnatural and horrible for us. In a way it's as if our souls are deprived of the oxygen they need to survive. Whether we like it or not we need relationship in order to survive.

So, how do we deal with this problem? How do we get through this season of being alone? How do we manage when it seems like the rest of the world is split off into couples…? Mmmmm… answers on a postcard…

But therein lies the problem as there is no magical answer. I am not here to tell you how not to feel lonely. I guess I am here to tell you that you can find God in the midst of it because that is what I have done.

Now, I don't want to contradict myself here but the ultimate cure for loneliness is not friendship. Ultimately the only cure for loneliness is love and the only way we truly find that love is through worship. I know that I have said the we were made for connection with one another and that God desired us to have people in our lives but there is a space in our hearts reserved for God alone and if we don't let Him in, then even if we were married tomorrow we would still be lonely; we could have all the friends in the world and we would still be lonely. This is best illustrated in the story of the woman at the well in John 4.

Once again she came to fill up her empty vessel. It was just a way of life by now. She'd fill it up then before she knew it emptiness came once again. She had no idea exactly how it happened or when the last moment of fulness was. But emptiness came once again. Five times she had done this. Five marriages, all failed. Every one promised so much, love, security, acceptance, happiness. But yet here she was again. Back at square one. She was now with Mr Number Six but already she knew it wasn't looking good so why even bother getting married this time. Her reputation was shot to pieces anyway so it didn't matter if she was living in sin. Now it was just a matter of getting through the day.

And the only thing that gets you through the day is routine. That's what we depend on when there is nothing else to hope for. We just do what we do. So what was on top of this woman's to-do list?

Water. Better get that water jar filled again.

So she made the familiar journey to the well. It was a well-worn path by now.

But who was this? She hadn't seen this Man before. He looked like a Jewish rabbi. What on earth was He doing here? Everyone knows the age-old argument which means that Jews have no dealings with Samaritans.

He even asked her for a drink. This is unprecedented.

He strikes up a conversation, talks about living water, and this strikes a chord within her. Is it possible that she could be so satisfied with this living water that she wouldn't have to keep coming to an empty well?

Hold on a second.

She can't let her guard down in front of a man. No way is she going to appear vulnerable to Him. She's done it before and it has never ended well. So she hides behind the veil of religious argument. That'll scare Him off. If He sees that she knows her religious blah blah blah then He'll think she's ok and leave her alone. She brings up the subject of worship and the right way to do it. Then He replies by saying that the day is coming when the true worshippers will worship in spirit and in truth. Woah! Truth? She doesn't like that word one little bit!

In essence He is saying, worship isn't something we do. It's who we are. The real us. This really scares her. Because she now sees herself as the empty vessel she really is. Then He cuts right to the chase. He asks her where her husband is. Now there's nowhere to hide. Before she even has time to answer, He answers - with the truth. Five husbands and now Mr Number Six, the shame of it.

But instead of feeling shame she feels something different - love. Real love. Not the empty love that she has been chasing all her life. She sees Him as the real deal. A speaker of truth - truth that sets her free. Free from wandering and wondering. Now she has met the source of all satisfaction. She is filled.

Companionship was not this woman's problem. She had the men queuing up to keep her company but yet she was still miserable. There was a well within her that was not being filled no matter how many of her own weddings she attended. You can hear it in her voice, "give me this water, that I may never come here to draw again" (John 4:15 NKJV).

She was tired. Tired of the same walk to the same well over and over again. Something had to change.

She was thirsty. Not satisfied.

Thirst drives us to do crazy things. When we are thirsty our vision is distorted. People in the desert become so thirsty that they see mirages of water in the distance and they run toward it only to realise all along it was sand. This woman had seen her share of mirages in the desert and was disappointed by all of them. But this meeting with Jesus was no mirage. It was the real thing.

What was Jesus' answer? Worship. Where marriage failed. Where even human companionship failed. Worship was the answer. Worship fills us right at the point of our emptiness, it puts God at the centre of our lives, then everything else we do revolves around that. He is the source. He has to come first. That's why we put worship beside us during our season on the shelf.

In the story Jesus tells us to worship in spirit and truth. Truth; this is a word we don't like. We often run away from the truth, yet Jesus is the truth. It says in the Bible that we shall know the truth and the truth will set us free (John 8:32). But somehow it's not the truth about Jesus that we don't like, it's the truth about ourselves. Just like that single woman at the well, she hid from the truth when Jesus confronted her with the truth of her own life.

Before we truly worship we have to get a revelation of truth, a revelation of the truth of Jesus, then out of that we will be able to face the truth about ourselves.

Just like the Samaritan woman, as single women, we need to have a revelation of the love of God. Why? Because if we don't understand how much He loves us then we will be relying on the love of every man we ever meet to fill that gap and no matter how good they are, how attentive they are, how many times they compliment us or how tight they hold our hand we will always be found wanting because these men are not Jesus.

All I am going to say is that Jesus loves you. Now you might think that is a bit of an obvious thing to say. I was brought up in a Christian home, I asked Jesus into my heart when I was a child, and I sang 'Jesus Loves Me' in church, but it is only in recent years that I have truly understood that He actually loved me.

There came a time when I started to wonder, if I realised how much God loved me then maybe I wouldn't worry so much, if I understood how much God loved me then maybe I wouldn't care so much about what other people think about me, if I understood how much he loved me then maybe I would like myself a little bit more.

All of these fears and insecurities amounted to a lack of understanding of God's love. As it says in 1 John 4:8, "God is love" (NKJV). So by not understanding the true meaning of love I was not understanding God himself, so how could I possibly worship someone I didn't completely understand?

In Eph 3:17, Paul encourages the Ephesian church "May you be rooted deep in love and founded securely on love" (AMP). This became my prayer and my personal mission which led me on a journey, not of self-discovery but of God discovery and of love discovery.

As a writer and communicator I feel very inadequate when it comes to talking about the love of God because if there was one sentence or phrase I could write to make you understand how much you are loved by Him I would write it, but there isn't. It has taken me years to comprehend that He loves me and even now I forget. I slip in and out of that assurance like a dream. I am constantly having to remind myself that He loves me because I forget so easily.

But you might be reading this thinking, "so what? Why is it so important to understand that we are loved?"

It is vitally important because love is the very foundation of our faith. The whole plan for our salvation was born out of love. It is because God so 'loved' the world that he gave us His Son. Paul prays for his church: " . . . may you be rooted deep in love and founded securely on love, that you may have the power and be strong to apprehend and grasp . . . what is the breadth and length and height and depth of it; that you may really come to know for yourselves – practically, through experience for yourselves – the love of Christ which far surpasses mere knowledge without experience" (Eph 3v17-19 AMP). That is what I am praying over you right now, as the reader of these words, that you would "have the power and be strong to apprehend and grasp" His love. His love is caught, not taught and so I must trust that you catch the love He has for you.

You may still be thinking, 'why do I have to understand this? Can I not just get on with my life without this earth-shattering revelation?' Well, the answer is 'yes,' and therein lies the danger. Many Christians have lived their lives without fully knowing His love, what that means for them and that is so sad as they have missed out on all that God has intended for them.

Just like the woman of Samaria they go to the well as part of their routine but are never fully satisfied.

We read in 1 John 4:8 that "God is love" (NKJV). If we replaced the word love in 1 Cor 13:1-3 with the word God, the first three verses would read something like this: "Though I speak with the tongues of men and of angels, but have not God, I have become a sounding brass or a clanging cymbal. And though I have the gift of prophecy, and understand all mysteries and all knowledge, and though I have all faith, so that I could remove mountains, but have not God, I am nothing. And though I bestow all my goods to feed the poor, and though I give my body to be burned, but have not God, it profits me nothing." Pretty shocking isn't it?

So, even though I was 'saved' I realised that I was missing out on a whole big chunk of God. How did I know? Because I was afraid I did a good job of hiding it but I was terrified. Of everything. Of the future, the past, what people thought of me, not being good enough. Everything. It was like fear was the cornerstone of my life.

I have often heard it said that faith is the opposite of fear but when I looked at my Bible I began to read these verses, "He who fears has not been made perfect in love" (1 Jn 4:18 NKJV). Notice that it doesn't say that they haven't been made perfect in 'faith' but 'love.' It doesn't say "perfect faith casts out fear" No, but rather "perfect love casts out fear" (1 Jn 4:18). I didn't need to work on my faith. I needed to be made perfect in love.

When I realised this I began a long, slow and at times painful journey toward that knowledge – the knowledge that I am perfectly loved. This is a journey I am still on and will be travelling for the rest of my life.

Half a person

When we are afraid of being known we can have people in our lives but still be very lonely as we constantly keep them at arms length. We can be invited to all the parties and yet be the loneliest person in the room. We can know hundreds yet be known by none. That is what makes us lonely.

When someone is married they often refer to their spouse as their 'other half.' This only perpetuates the lie that we are sold in this culture that whilst we are single we are only half a person. That is why there is such emphasis on being a part of a couple and almost a panic when this doesn't work out for you.

Now I don't want to offend anyone in what they believe but I refuse to marry half a man and I refuse to be half a woman for the man I'm going to marry. I want us to already be whole when we come together. Now please note, I am not saying perfect, just whole.

There is a difference. Perfection is unattainable this side of Heaven, but I believe we can grow into wholeness. How? By growing in the revelation of the love of God.

The point is that this revelation will change your life. It will change how you live your life, it will change how you see God, it will change how you believe God sees you. When you see yourself as loved, never again will you see yourself as abandoned or rejected. As a single woman you will be able to face this season of aloneness without fear because you will be assured that God is in control. You will know that He has the times and seasons in His hands.

At times when I was most lonely, instead of running from God in anger or bitterness at the state I was in, I've learned to draw close to Him because I knew He was the only one who would get me through it. God spoke to me through Luke 10:38-42. It's the story of when Jesus visited Mary and Martha, the sisters of Lazarus, and how "Mary also sat at Jesus' feet and heard His word" (v39). He showed me that this was me. This was my place, this is where I belonged. As long as I could always see myself sitting at the feet of Jesus in a position of worship and hearing His Word then everything else in my life would fit around that. That understanding would give perspective to everything else that would happen in my life. Jesus said that Mary had found the "good part" that would not "be taken away from her" (v42 NKJV). Time and time again in those seasons of loneliness I make myself go to that place and I have found that "good part." I haven't always felt like it but in those times when I felt lost and alone and like I didn't belong anywhere or with anyone, I go back to His feet. Sometimes I have to drag myself there, but as soon as I get there I know I am home again. This is where I can be myself and not be ashamed. This is where I am accepted just as I am. This is where I can begin to see truth and begin fighting Satan and his lies. I know here that I am not alone because I am with the One Who will never leave me or forsake me. I pray that you find that place in God. I pray that He becomes your "refuge and strength, a very present help in trouble" (Psa 46:1 NKJV).

Known by love

The peculiar thing about being lonely is that you kind of get used to it. When I think of meeting someone and allowing them to become a part of my life I get excited and terrified all at the same time. It is not the effort of getting to know someone but the fact that I have to allow them to get to know me. I have to let them see all my flaws and failures and weaknesses and all the other things I work so hard at hiding. I suppose what I suffer from is a fear of being known, but I am so thankful for a verse in 1 Cor 13 that says: "but then I shall know just as I also am known." (v12 NKJV). This verse is referring to the full revelation of God's love and how someday we shall truly know God as today we can only see through a dim mirror. Its describes how we will know clearly just as God knows us clearly here and now.

Excuse me? He knows me now? As I am right now?

It was another story about another woman at another well that helped me understand how much I was loved. This story is found in Genesis 16. It is the story of Hagar, the maidservant of Sarah and Abraham. Abraham had received a promise from God that he and Sarah would bear a son - but they were a little impatient so they decided to take a shortcut which is never a good idea when it comes to obeying God! Hagar was one of their female servants so

Sarah suggested that Hagar become a surrogate mother and become pregnant by Abraham. This happened quickly and as soon as Hagar was pregnant, Sarah became bitterly resentful and began misusing and abusing Hagar to such an extent that Hagar was left with no other option but to run away. Genesis 16:6 says, "Sarah dealt harshly with her [Hagar] and she fled from her presence" (NKJV).

Try to imagine Hagar's position as she wandered through a barren wilderness afraid, confused, lonely, misunderstood, physically weak and emotionally tormented. Abraham and Sarah were so consumed with their own lives that they never once took her wellbeing into consideration. They were most likely feeling guilty for disobeying God's plan and were projecting that guilt onto Hagar. She had put herself on the line for them and they didn't even give her the appreciation she was due. She had become invisible to them. She had no other option but to leave.

So she wandered until she came to a well. It must have been a hot day and she was thirsty - in every way it was possible to be thirsty. At least her physical thirst could be quenched here. Little did she

74

know that her every need would be met at this well. For, just like the woman from Samaria, she too would have an encounter with Someone who could satisfy. She met an Angel that day, a messenger from God, who was able to tell Hagar her past but more importantly her future. By the end of their encounter Hagar had a whole new perspective on life.

She named that well Beer-Lah-Roi, literally 'the well of the One who lives and sees me.' She knew that she was no longer invisible. She may have been unseen by Abraham and Sarah and the rest of the world but she was seen by the Most High. He saw her struggle, her pain, her mess and her despair.

He saw.

That was all she needed to know - that He saw her just as she was right there and then.

We all need to visit that well. I needed to visit that well. It was vital that I knew that God saw me just as I was. But I was so afraid of being seen. That is why I had such a hard time comprehending His love. True love involves intimacy and intimacy means that you are seen.

Love is not blind
Love sees
And loves
Despite what it sees.

I was someone who covered up my entire life. I was very proud of the fact that no one ever really knew me. Different people knew different parts but no one person knew it all. Until I came to the well, then I realised that He saw me. His love saw it all. Every time I said 'ok' when I wasn't. Every physical struggle, every emotional pain, I may have hidden it from the world but the Creator of the world saw it all and He cared about it all. Every disappointment, every question, every heartbreak. Nothing was hidden from His sight.

Hagar asked after her encounter, "Have I also seen here the One who sees me?" (Gen 6:13). I asked the same question, and for both myself and Hagar the answer was 'yes.' I knew that He was the One who healed me, strengthened me and led me. However before

He could be any of those things I had to allow Him to be the One who saw me. I had to drink from that well before I could go any further in my journey.

I did drink from that well, and as I allowed Him to see me for all that I was then I began to see Him for all he was, a God of love, grace, peace, strength, wisdom, and the list goes on and on. The revelation of Him goes on and on for all my life until that final revelation when I reach my home in Heaven and see Him face to face.

Please take time to drink from this well. Allow Him to see you as you are, no masks, no Sunday-best outfits.

Just you.

Really I have no need to be afraid of being known as I am already known by my Creator yet He still chooses to love me. It is this knowledge that makes me secure and a little more whole on the inside.

PART 3

Placing Friendship on the Shelf

"Entreat Me Not To Leave You" (Ruth 1:16).

"I'll be there for you, when the rain starts to fall...." Of course we all know that song. It's the theme song for the hit comedy series, 'Friends.' I was a massive fan and loved watching the lives of Rachel, Phoebe, Monica, Joey, Chandler and Ross unfold in the Central Perk in New York. I loved how they were there for each other no matter what and how they remained friends throughout the varying seasons of their life.

It was great to watch on TV but I never really felt that I had that in my own life. The usual story, I trusted, I got hurt, I vowed never to trust again. So instead of building bridges, I built walls. Big thick walls that no one could get through. But those walls that were meant to protect me only isolated me. Then I wondered why I was lonely.

Yet I know that friendship is a vital part in all of our lives and I believe we can grow from it whether our experiences are negative or positive.

When God told me to put friendship on my shelf I wasn't so sure. I thought I could do without it and that me and God would be enough. Sadly, I was wrong, so in order to write this part of the book and fill this part of the shelf I've had to go on a real journey. I have had to look at what constitutes a godly friendship. I had to find out what the Bible has to say about the subject. I have asked the people around me what they think about friendship and what issues they have struggled with in their experience. Most importantly I've had to face my fears of friendship and allow myself to love and be loved in this way. I have had to put myself back in the firing line and learn to trust, be vulnerable and confess my weaknesses, sins and hang-ups to another human being. This is incredibly scary and it hasn't always worked out perfectly but those friendships that God has ordained have made my life richer and stronger and I can't imagine my life without them.

I thank God for the people who weren't afraid of my walls but helped me knock them down brick by brick. These people know who they are.

This part of the Shelf is dedicated to them xx.

Jesus, Friend of Sinners

So why should we even put friendship on our shelf? After all, isn't the point of this book to encourage us to be happier as we are and in ourselves and in our relationship with God? Why add people into the mix to complicate things?

I cannot tell you how many times I have wished that could be the case. One day God and I could be walking along fine – then BAM! Someone comes in and upsets the equilibrium. How dare they spoil my alone time with my Creator!

But no matter how much I have protested, God seems to allow this to happen. It is as if He wants me to share my life with the people around me. I just cannot understand it, and every time I try to do this I keep making a mess of it.

To quote a well used cliché: "What doesn't kill you makes you stronger." If that's the case then this has to be the strongest part of my life because it feels like I have been lying bleeding on the ground many times now and it is only by the grace of God I have been able to get back up.

However, for this section I'm not just going to spout from my wisdom. I am flawed, I am sure you have been able to work that out long before now, but there is One person Who walked this earth Who wasn't flawed, and He had friends. Yes, Jesus, Friend of sinners, and also a bunch of other ragamuffins.

Jesus was God's representative on earth, He had direct access to the Father, yet He did not complete His earthly journey alone. He chose to surround Himself with companions. Yes, I know in the Bible, a formal title of 'disciples' is placed on these men but Jesus called them his friends (John 5:13-15). I cannot help but think of the times of friendship these people had as they travelled all over Israel in that day. They went to people's houses for dinner along with tax collectors and other such crooks. If they had been so dull why would all of these people have magnetically gathered around them. You have to admit that even in these social networking days of Twitter and Facebook its hard to gather a spontaneous crowd of 5000, never mind back in those days when all people had to rely on was word of mouth. So these guys had something dynamic that drew people to them, and that could only have been born out of a genuine friendship.

From a young age Jesus knew He had to be about His Father's business (Luke 2:49). He had a sense of who He was and this is why He was able to be the "friend of tax collectors and sinners" (Matt 11:19 NKJV). As I have studied Jesus' interaction with the people around Him I have noticed a few things that can help us in our friendships. Lets look at how He related to the people around Him.

- He did not depend on them for His identity.

When He was baptised by John the Baptist, a voice from Heaven sounded and said, "This is My beloved Son in Whom I am well pleased" (Matt 3:17 NKJV). This gave Jesus all the acceptance, identity and approval that He needed so Jesus didn't need to look for it in the people around Him. He knew that His Father loved Him and approved of Him so He didn't need to go around looking to others to fill that need.

It is a good thing that Jesus received this confirmation at this time, immediately after His baptism He went into the wilderness and the first thing Satan brought into question for Jesus was his identity. He said "If you are the Son of God..." Immediately Jesus' authority was questioned through questioning His identity. When you are unsure of your identity you can't be sure of anything else in your life, but thankfully Jesus knew who He was and was able to defeat Satan at every point of testing.

John 13:1-5: "Now before the Feast of the Passover, when Jesus knew that His hour had come that He should depart from this world to the Father, having loved His own who were in the world, He loved them to the end. And supper being ended, the devil having already put it into the heart of Judas Iscariot, Simon's son, to betray Him, Jesus, knowing that the Father had given all things into His hands, and that He had come from God and was going to God, rose from supper and laid aside His garments, took a towel and girded Himself. After that, He poured water into a basin and began to wash the disciples' feet, and to wipe them with the towel with which He was girded" (NKJV).

This passage describes the night that Jesus washed His disciples'
feet. This is the greatest act of servanthood we see in Scripture
and should be the example we all follow in friendship. How could
Jesus, the Son of God perform such a lowly act? Could you? I
believe the key is found in verse 3: "Jesus, knowing that the Father
had given all things into His hands, and that He had come from God
and was going to God." Jesus had complete security, not in the
people around Him but in His Father and Who his Father created
Him to be.

I get so mad at myself for the times I rely on the people around me
for my identity. I think the status of the people around me will rub off
onto me so I try to schmooze with the great and the good. It starts
with all of us in childhood, we want to be the popular kid or at least
be friends with the popular kid, and so the cycle continues
throughout our lives. It's what I like to call, 'The it's not what you
know, it's who you know syndrome.' I am definitely a sufferer.
That's way too much pressure for any friendship, it has got nothing
to do with who I know but everything to do with what I know. And
what should that be? That I am loved, accepted, called by my

Father in heaven. Once I have a full revelation of that I will have no problem in rising up, laying aside everything I use to cover myself up and serving the people in my world.

- Jesus did not choose people who were like Him.

He did not pick twelve carpenters to follow Him. He chose from a wide variety of characters and backgrounds including men and women, quiet and loud. He chose hard-working, honest fishermen, then he chose a dodgy tax-collector. He loved spending time in the house of Mary and Martha, sisters who frequently disagreed. Then there was Mary Magdalene, a woman with a questionable reputation, from whom He had cast out seven demons.

What am I trying to say here? Mix it up. Don't try to be friends with people who are exactly like you. How dull! The best friendships I have in my life are the ones that took me by surprise. I am now closest to people with whom I have nothing in common! One of my best friends is ten years older than me (sorry, Tracy!) married with two children. She lives about an hour away from me and we only get to see each other about once a month on average. Our lives could not be more different yet we frequently finish each other's sentences. We have been through the best and worst of times together and I know that we will be friends for life. All my life I wanted a best friend who was exactly like me, someone who was my age, single and lived nearby so we could hang out all the time but it never happened. I would become friendly with people and think, 'This is the one,' but it was always the wrong person and it would end up in disaster. Then I gave up trying make it happen. That is when God took control and gave me the friends He wanted me to have all along and not the friends I thought I should have. He has done this time and time again, hooked me up with people I would never have thought likely friends but they are so dear to me now my life would be so much poorer without them.

I cannot wait to see who else God is going to put on the Shelf beside me and what we will accomplish together.

- Jesus did not depend on them for approval.

"Jesus came to a town one day and He said that He could do no mighty works there because the people didn't believe in Him" (Mark

6:5 NKJV). So He left. He didn't stay and try to convince them how wonderful He was. He didn't force Himself on those people. I have no doubt that he wanted desperately to heal the people in that place but as they were determined not to allow Him near, He respected that and moved on, secure in Himself and His mission.

You have to realise that some people are just not going to get you. No matter how much you want to be bosom buddies with them they just won't feel the same and the last thing you should do is force a friendship. I have tried and it has been disastrous every time.

Please note: there is a fine line to tread. Friendship requires effort and you don't always get an immediate return on your investment but there does come a time when you have to stand back and ask yourself, "is this worth my while?" This may seem like a contradiction to what I said in my previous point about being in friendship not for what you get but for what you can give and this is true to a degree. If you feel like you are the one doing all the work and putting in all the effort and you know it is not appreciated like it should be, then pull back.

- Jesus allowed himself to care deeply for them.

"Jesus wept" (John 11:35 NKJV). The shortest verse in the Bible, yet one of the most powerful. It gives us a real insight into the humanity of Jesus. He wasn't weeping over the whole world or even the nation of Israel as you might expect from the Son of God. He was crying at the death of His friend, Lazarus. Even though He was on His way to raise him from the dead, He allowed Himself to grieve and feel the loss of a friend. It shows that He allowed Himself to care, that He put himself in a position where He could feel emotional pain. It shows that He truly was touched by the feelings of our infirmities (Heb 4:15), not just our physical infirmities but our emotional weaknesses. He missed His friend. This is the God of the whole universe allowing Himself to feel at a loss because the friend that He created in the first place, had gone. Jesus allowed Himself to be at a loss. I find this incredible.

One of the reasons friendships do not work as they should is because we are not prepared to do this. We do not want anyone to have that kind of power over us. We refuse to be vulnerable to that extent. It is hard to put yourself out there especially when you have been hurt in the past but until you do true friendship cannot exist for you. After the terrible atrocity of 9/11 in New York Queen Elizabeth made a speech and in it she said, "Grief is the price we pay for love." If we want the true love of friendship we must be prepared to face true grief if that friendship ever ends.

- Jesus was never disillusioned by them.

It was the night before the crucifixion. The worst night of Jesus' life. The night when He needed His friends the most. Yet what were they doing? At best they were sleeping and at worst they were denying and betraying Him. But none of this shocked Jesus. In fact, He foretold it to them, Matt 26:31 says, "All of you will be made to stumble because of Me this night (NKJV)." However, despite all this knowledge and disappointment He didn't stop loving them.

Face facts, your friends have limits. They're going to hurt you and let you down. They're going to have quirks and idiosyncrasies that get right on your nerves but do not let that stop you from loving them...and don't let that stop them from loving you.

"Let me in!"

Twitter, Facebook, texting, Skype, Facetime, everybody seems to be chatting nowadays, but is anyone really talking? Or is anyone really listening?

It's great to have a laugh with someone and catch up over coffee. It's good to post on someone's wall and say, "Hey how are you doing?" And it's good to reply by saying, "Hey, I'm fine." But that doesn't really constitute deep friendship does it? How can you really tell someone what's going on in your life in 140 characters? Friendship is much more than that.

It is easy today to know a lot of people but ironically it is harder to get to know them, and it is harder to let them get to know you. Do you understand what I mean? We are so busy replying to texts and emails, tweeting and face-booking that we never really let anyone in. At least, that was my problem.

The following few paragraphs are words that I wrote to some people in my world a few years ago. It is by far one of the scariest things I have ever done, but I had to do it.

The Room and the Door

All my life I've sat in a room and it felt lonely all by myself. But recently some people have stopped at the door and we've got talking, but you can only get so close to someone when there's a door between you. My mistake was that I thought the lock was on the other side of the door and it was up to people to open the door and when that didn't happen I felt rejected and angry that I was still in the room on my own.

But I now realise that the lock was on my side. The whole time it was up to me to open the door and let them in. But I am so used being in this room on my own that the thought of people coming in kind of scares me. It's my room, I am safe here. What if they don't like the room? What if they mess it up? What if they don't come into the room after I have taken the massive step of opening the door in the first place? What if they come into the room and then leave?

This is what is running through my mind as I turn the key.

So come in, don't come in, leave the room if you want.

The door is open.

Writing this left me feeling so vulnerable, but that is what constitutes true friendship.

The practice of leaving yourself bare for people to see inside of you, see the worst of you and still believe the best.

Do you have people in your life whom you can communicate with on that level or are your friendships all very pleasant, 'Hey how are you? Hey, I'm fine, thanks' kind of friendships?

So after I sent the writing about 'The Room and the Door' to my friends did my room get messed up? Most definitely, yes. Did some people not come into the room at all? Yes. Did some people walk into the room and walk back out again? Yes. But some

94

people came into the room and they stayed. These people are my best friends.

I got some surprises when I opened the door. Some people I expected to come in didn't come in and some of the people who stayed are the ones I least expected.

You will be surprised once you open the door.

Remember, **you** have to open the door. Some of you are like me, feeling sad and lonely and not a little angry because no one has yet entered your room, but remember you have the key. What does that key look like? For me it was writing that email and sending it out to those people in my life. For you it may be more simple. Maybe turning the key for you is the next time someone asks you how you are, instead of smiling and saying, 'hey, I'm fine,' you need be honest and say how you really are.

Being brave is not always a good thing, being brave can make for a lonely existence. Take it from an expert. Living life from a wheelchair, the most common attitude I encountered from people was sympathy. They just looked at me and said, "Awwwwww." This drove me crazy. So I have always felt the need to prove people wrong and never show how I struggled. I was good at this, even from childhood, so much so that at the age of ten I was given a Child of Courage Award because I was so brave. That was cute when I was ten years old but when I was hitting thirty and God was speaking to me about true friendship and letting people in, it just made me lonely.

James 5:16 says, "Confess your trespasses to one another, and pray for one another, that you may be healed" (NKJV). I also had to allow others to see me in a mess. I had to learn to cry on other people's shoulders. But this has brought more healing and I am slowly learning that it's okay to not be okay. The trespasses talked about in James 5 are not just your sins, I believe they include your weaknesses and all the stuff you try to hide from people. It says that healing, not forgiveness, comes from doing this. God is the only one who can forgive your sins but healing comes when you share that deep, dark part of you with someone and you realise that they love and accept you in spite of that. This is what I had to do. Slowly I began to lift the lid and understand that it was okay not to be okay, and to let other people see me not be okay. Let us have a look at Ruth and Naomi's friendship. This is exactly how it was with them.

Ruth and Naomi

You are Ruth, and you need someone to look up to. You need to cling to someone who can take you to the place you need to be. There are people around you who God has placed there for you to follow and learn from. I thank God for every Naomi in my life, those inspiring and awesome women who have led the way and made my journey a little easier by giving me their wisdom.

For every Ruth there is hope in finding a Naomi.

They had been through so much together, so many happy times, so many sad times. Is that not what true friendship is? Shared memories both good and bad. Yet Naomi also had these memories with her other daughter-in-law, Orpah, yet Orpah turned back from Naomi and Ruth to start a new life. Who could blame her?

So why was Ruth different? It is obvious that the bond between Ruth and Naomi was forged by more than just shared memories. The bond between them went much deeper than that. God was in the mix. It says in Ecc 4:12: "A cord of three strands is not quickly broken (NIV)." This verse is often applied to marriage but it can also be relevant to friendship. When our friendships become God focused and based on His purpose they can become a powerful force for good.

This verse is never more true than when it is read in the context of Ruth and Naomi. Ruth's relationship with Orpah was only two stranded. They had shared experiences but no shared faith and vision. Therefore when crunch time came, the friendship fell apart. There was nothing holding them together. Have you found that in friendships? It is all very nice but there comes a time when things change and decisions need to be made. The friendship either moves on to another level or it just fizzles out.

This has happened to me a few times and when I was younger I carried around a lot of guilt because I felt I had left people behind. Now I know that they were never intended by God to be part of my future and that if I had held on they would have slowed me down or taken me in a direction I should not have gone. Can you imagine if Ruth and Naomi had allowed Orpah to direct them? Their whole fate would have been re-defined and I doubt that there would have been a book of Ruth in the Bible today. This story of redemption would have been lost.

Ruth was different. She weaved God into the fabric of her friendship. She cried out, "Your God shall be my God." She made Him that extra 'cord' which meant the friendship wasn't 'easily broken'. The strongest friendships in my life are the ones where God has been woven in and He is what holds us together. There is grace in that cord, grace to allow us to be who we are without apology. You cannot be in a friendship with someone if you feel you cannot truly be who you are. Grace gives you the freedom to be you and for the other person to be who they are. There is also purpose in that cord. You will be drawn together because of the purpose God has placed within you.

A perfect example of this in Scripture is the story of Mary and Elizabeth. When Mary became pregnant with our Messiah she went to visit her cousin Elizabeth who at the same time was also pregnant with John the Baptist. When Mary greeted Elizabeth it says that "the babe leaped in her womb" (Luke 1:41 NKJV) and Elizabeth was filled with the Holy Spirit. This is such a picture of purpose in friendship. Here were two women both carrying something God-given and whenever they got together something amazing happened, something supernatural! What was inside Elizabeth reacted to what was inside Mary and boom! Have you encountered someone and what is inside of you explodes because of what is inside them? That is purpose my friend! It will entwine itself between the two of you and take you on a journey you never thought possible, just like Ruth and Naomi.

Let me ask you - who is guiding you? Is it Orpah or Naomi? You will have both types of people in your life and the choice is yours as to who you follow. Orpah will take you back. Back to familiar territory back to the place where people just expect you to be the person you've always been. Orpah did not want things to be different however, we cannot live life like that. There comes a point in your life where you cannot stay the same, you are either moving forward or going backwards. The story of Lot's wife in the Bible confirms this. In Genesis 19 Abraham's bother, Lot, and his wife were living in Sodom, one of the cities God had identified for judgement but Abraham prayed to God that He would have mercy on his family and that they would be spared. Angels were sent to the city to rescue Lot and his family, but as they were escaping the city, Lot's wife looked back to Sodom as it was being destroyed and she became a pillar of salt. So sad. She was made aware of the freedom that was hers, but she didn't embrace the truth. She thought she could live her life as it always was. But she was wrong.

Don't be like Lot's wife. Embrace the truth. Let it set you free and take you to the place God has intended for you. Will it mean change? Most definitely! Will it be easy? Definitely not! But it will be worth it.

This moment came for me in 2006 in a market in Covent Garden, London. I was over there with my family celebrating my Mum's 60th birthday. We had gone shopping in the market and I came across a picture with these words written on it:

"Our deepest fear is not that we are inadequate. Our deepest fear is that we are powerful beyond measure. It is our light, not our darkness that most frightens us. We ask ourselves, Who am I to be brilliant, gorgeous, talented, fabulous? Actually, who are you not to be? You are a child of God. Your playing small does not serve the world. There is nothing enlightened about shrinking so that other people won't feel insecure around you. We are all meant to shine, as children do. We were born to make manifest the glory of God that is within us. It's not just in some of us; it's in everyone. And as we let our own light shine, we unconsciously give other people permission to do the same. As we are liberated from our own fear, our presence automatically liberates others" (Marriane Williamson).

After I read that I was out of excuses. I knew I had to change and be the person God created me to be. I had to stop hiding. I saw the truth. But I had to decide what to do with it. I could have read those words that day and turned away but I'm pretty sure that if I had done that I wouldn't be writing these words now.

Once you have been made aware of the truth you have a responsibility as to what you do with it. Will you allow it to change you? Or will you turn your back. You may think that you can just continue to be the same but that is not the case.

But Naomi will take you forward into the land of the unknown, into a place where you will have to step up and allow yourself to be stretched. Into a place where you will have to encounter situations that will change you and help you become the woman God created you to be and fulfil the purpose God created you for.

You are Naomi.

You have been on a journey and have come through some tough stuff that you don't quite understand, If you look around you will see Ruth clinging to you, begging to come with you on your journey as she is lost without you. You are her only hope for a better future as only you know the way to the land of promise. Will you lead her? Will you set aside your own problems and grief and take her by the hand and lead her to her destiny?

For every Naomi there is a responsibility in being confronted with Ruth.

Up until now I have spent all of this chapter speaking of Ruth the young woman with her life ahead of her so full of expectation and promise.

There are people reading this and you are not like Ruth. You are a Naomi. You have lived your life and, like the woman we read of in the book of Ruth, your life has not turned out the way you had imagined. Now you find yourself at a crossroads feeling nothing but the bitterness that Naomi felt.

The question on your lips is 'why?'

Why did that happen?
Why did that not happen?
Why me?
Why not me?

I have asked all those same questions at some point

In the midst of your grief there is someone standing behind you, her name is Ruth. Despite what you may think of yourself and the state of your life she has seen something in you that she wants. She wants your God to be her God. Will you allow her to embrace you? Will you introduce her to your God? Will you take her to the 'House of Bread' and show her the way to her destiny? There are Ruths everywhere in the body of Christ crying for Naomi to do this. Can you set aside your questions and your grief just to nurture her? Can you realise that your best days are not behind you? If you embrace Ruth she will lead you to your destiny also. To be a woman of wisdom and counsel, raising up a generation of women to follow God.

By looking at Ruth and Naomi we see the purpose that comes from true friendship. If you get over your issues around friendship you will see it is not about you but about the purpose God wants to accomplish through you.

Now, let's have a closer look at purpose...

PART 4

Placing Purpose on the Shelf

"Let me go to the field." (Ruth 2:2)

Purpose - I've always known I've had one. I don't know why.
Maybe it's something to do with the fact that on the 20th of October
1978 the doctors told my parents that I wouldn't live or if I did I
wouldn't have much of a life due to the severe disabilities I was
born with. But God had the final say and He healed me and kept
me alive for a reason.

Part of that reason is you. God kept me alive because He knew
that a book needed to be written and you needed to read it so this
part of my shelf is dedicated to you.

I pray you become as aware of your purpose as I am of mine xx.

Ruth's Purpose

We've seen Ruth's worship in choosing God over the Moabite idols, and her friendship in her embracing of Naomi. In addition, we have the luxury of knowing the end of the story.

At the end of the book of Ruth a genealogy is written. It shows how Ruth gave birth to the man who would be the grandfather of King David: "Then Naomi took the child and laid him in her lap, and became his nurse. The neighbour women gave him a name, saying, 'A son has been born to Naomi!' So they named him Obed. He is the father of Jesse, the father of David. Now these are the generations of Perez: to Perez was born Hezron, and to Hezron was born Ram, and to Ram, Amminadab, and to Amminadab was born Nahshon, and to Nahshon, Salmon, and to Salmon was born Boaz, and to Boaz, Obed, and to Obed was born Jesse, and to Jesse, David" (Ruth 4:16-22 NASB).

Jesus came from that same lineage.

We see in Matthew 1 that Ruth is one of only four women to be mentioned in the lineage of Christ. To be part of that family tree is pretty awesome and it shows how important Ruth's purpose was, but as I said at the beginning of this chapter, we know the end of the story. Ruth had no idea of this purpose for her life. We know the big picture but Ruth was caught up in the small details. All she knew was that she and Naomi would starve if she didn't go and get them some food. So she got up from her loneliness and lack and resolved to do what it took to feed herself and Naomi. In Ruth chapter 2 she declares to her bitter mother-in-law, "Let me go to the field" Ruth 2:2 NIV). She didn't know the future, she just decided to be faithful to the woman who had shown her love. But this small act of faithfulness was the first step she took on her road to purpose.

Maybe you feel like Ruth did way back then.

"What's the point? What's the plan? Is there a plan? I've been on a roller coaster journey up until this point but what now?" May I suggest that you follow Ruth's example. Learn the long-lost art of faithfulness. Find the field that is in front of you and go there. You might not see how this is in any way relevant to what God has put on your heart but you will be surprised where faithfulness can lead you.

You see, there is a journey between what's in your heart and what's in your hand, and the road between the two is called faithfulness. Time after time in Scripture we see how people of purpose have had to make this journey and walk this road. One of my favourite examples is that of David. Over the years I have taken so much comfort from his story, He is one person who really shows us how to be faithful with what is in our hands whilst we are waiting for God to fulfil what is in our hearts.

David was a young boy when Samuel the prophet came to anoint him as King over Israel (1 Sam 16). Now, you would think after that ceremony, after he was "anointed ... in the presence of his brothers" (1 Sam 16:13 NIV) that David's life would have changed dramatically. You would think that David's brothers would be bowing before him and serving him in any way they could, but this is not the case. We see that after David was anointed King nothing changed for him. In the next chapter, where Goliath is taunting the Israelite army, the only reason David ends up at that field is because he is delivering food to his brothers on the battlefield. Remember - he is anointed King but here he is working as a lunch boy.

David knows there is so much more he could do but here he is delivering the bread and cheese. Have you ever had days like that? I've had more than my fair share - knowing God had placed something inside of me but it seemed at that moment in time all I was doing was delivering the 'bread and cheese' - I was caught up in 'stuff' that didn't seem in any way related to what God had placed in my heart. I mean, put yourself in David's position, what did the bread and cheese in his hands have to do with leading his nation into freedom; that's what was in his heart, that was his destiny. Doing the lunch run was a far cry from that, but David walked the road of faithfulness and that day when his father asked him to take the food to his brothers, David didn't turn his nose up in horror of being asked to do such a menial task. He went down to the field, lunch box in hand, and that act of obedience positioned him for destiny. If David had allowed pride to get in the way of his service he wouldn't have been on hand when it came to defeating Goliath. He had to walk the road of faithfulness by faith - he had the freedom of his people in his heart but he had bread and cheese in his hand. How could the two ever be linked? How could one ever lead to the other? But they were linked. If it hadn't been for him carrying the bread and cheese he would never have been in position to defeat Goliath.

Moses had the same struggle between his heart and hand. His heart was full of desire to see his people set free. In Exodus 2 it says that Moses looked on his people with compassion and was moved to action, albeit it was the wrong kind of action as it ended up with him committing murder and having to flee Egypt. Nevertheless he had freedom in his heart but he ended up with a shepherd's crook in his hand. It would be easy to feel that he had missed his chance. How could his rod ever help bring freedom to his people? Yet, we should never count ourselves as finished in the purposes of God. You'd be amazed at how God can use what is in your hand to fulfil what is in your heart. That rod which Moses carried in the desert to herd a few sheep became known as the 'staff of God' and it was used to perform miracle after miracle that led to the freedom of the people of Israel.

For years I knew God had called me to share His truth. I had a passion for His word and communicating it to people, but I wasn't always in the place to do this. I had a battle going on inside of me - a battle between what was in my hand and what was in my heart and at times it seemed the two couldn't have been further removed from each other. I have had more than my fair share of things in my hand and at times I have struggled to see the connection with my heart but all along God was there testing my heart by seeing if I could be faithful with what was in my hand. Some days I passed that test and some days I failed but God was faithful even when I was not and he was patient and waited until I saw the value of faithfulness in even the smallest of things. It is those small things that have allowed me to get to where I am now.

God looks for our faithfulness where no one else can see it or appreciate it. It is a bit like a support act on tour with the headline act. It comes on stage and no one there has paid to see it. Everyone is there to see the main act! Yet the performers have to go on stage and sing the songs they were meant to sing with as much effort and gusto as the headliners, the only thing is no one in the audience knows the words. They have to sing their song to a silent audience who are really wishing they would get off the stage so they can listen to the person they paid to hear. The support act has to sing their song even when no one else is singing along.

Can you do that? Are you able to faithfully do what he has called you without the applause and approval of the people around you? Can you sing the song He has given you without anybody else singing along? God will never allow you to become the main attraction if you cannot be a faithful support act. Look at the people we have talked about:

• David was destined to be King over all of Israel but before that he was tested in how he delivered the lunch to his obnoxious brothers.
• Moses was destined to be the deliverer of his people but before that he was tested in rounding up a few sheep in the desert.
• Ruth was destined to be a part of a royal lineage but before that she was tested in how she gathered the harvest in the field.

So far I've written about people who knew what their call was - or at least had a strong sense. David knew he was meant to be king,

Moses maybe didn't know exactly what he was meant to do but he had a strong desire for the freedom of his people. Maybe you have no idea what God has called you to do or even if he has called you to do anything at all.

Let me clear up a few things for you. If you are alive on planet earth today then you are here for a purpose. God is crazy about you and He loves you so much He would love you to be with Him for eternity in Heaven, but He needs you to be here on earth just for a little while in order to fulfil a plan He needs carried out. Psalm 139:16 says, "In Your book they were written, the days fashioned for me when as yet there were none of them" (KJV). Whether you believe it or not God had this very day planned for you before you even took your first breath. He knew you would pick up this book and read these words. He knew you would be sitting right where you are sitting. In fact these words that you are reading were written before I was even born and able to write them!! Eph 2:10 says, "He has created us for good works that he has prepared beforehand that we should walk in them" (KJV). This tells me that He created the works - the purpose - before He created us. In fact He custom made us to fit the purpose - not the other way around.

We are a designer product made to fit the purpose for our lives. How can we say we have no purpose?

Killing the White

I see my calling much like the book spoken of in Psalm 139. I believe my book is written up in Heaven but it seems like God sent me here with a blank copy and it's my job to fill each of those pages. Everything I do, every 'yes', every 'no' is a sentence in that book. Every person who is touched by the words I write or say is a paragraph. Every blog post, every word spoken in encouragement is a page in that book. When I reach heaven I can just imagine God and I sitting down and comparing notes. It is my hope and prayer that as we do so there will be as few discrepancies as possible.

What about your book? Do you even know you have one? God is leaning over your already-written book in heaven. He has written an amazing story and he is longing for you to live it. He is willing you to pick up the pen and begin filling the blank pages he has assigned to you down here. Blank pages are scary, I know. I'm a writer and I spend most of my days staring at one. They scream at me, "You'll never fill me! Who do you think you are? You'll never make a mark on me." Every day I have to silence that voice by writing something. It doesn't matter if it's good or bad, I just have to kill that white, screaming space in front of me. Even in the writing of this book I have written everything many times. The first time, I wrote something just to put something on the page. To silence the space, to kill the white. Most of the time it was terrible, but at least there was something on the page. Then I could go back and edit it. I added words that hadn't been written. I removed words that were written. I changed the order of paragraphs. It was easier because I had something to work with. I had to give myself permission the first time around to not produce perfect prose. I had to allow myself to have flaws in my writing.

I can imagine there is a blank page screaming at you. Maybe it's not an actual page like mine, but maybe it's a career, an idea, a friendship and it is staring at you. You know you have words to write, but you are terrified of making a mistake. All I can say to you is write. Write something, anything, make a mark. You may have to go back and make adjustments, you may have to add something that you left out or subtract something that really shouldn't be there, but that's okay. You need to give yourself permission not to get it right first time. Just understand that God will give you the grace to go back and change things, but go ahead - make that call, approach that person, apply for that course - the page is silenced. You have written a sentence in your book. Well done.

The Daughters of Thunder

Now I hate to be a spoil sport but while you begin writing your book you will encounter struggle like you've never known. Satan will do all in his power to stop you from putting pen to paper. There will be days when you want to quit. But in those moments when there seems to be no way forward you must remember that you are not the only person who will read what you write. Your book becomes the inspiration for other people who will read you and they will say, "if she can do it I can do it."

The one phrase that drives me is, "Its not about me." I have used this one thought to get myself through the toughest of times. There have been certain things in my life that have not made sense. I have questions, but I have realised that my struggle is not necessarily about me in that moment. Yes there is an immediate battle to be won but there is also a bigger picture. Your battle and struggle is making way for the people around you. They will see you and draw comfort and courage from your life. God has chosen you to fight a battle and win it so that others don't have to fight it.

Let me tell you a story about a group of women who fully understood that there were people coming after them that would be affected directly by their actions. In scripture they are known as the Daughters of Zelophehad. Their names are Mahlah, Noah, Hoglah, Milcah and Tirzah but I like to call them 'The Daughters of Thunder'. Why? Jesus called two brothers, James and John, in his group of disciples 'The Sons of Thunder' because of their strength and tenacity. These women are a feisty bunch of single ladies who weren't afraid to stand up and fight for their rights.

Their story is found in Numbers 27:1-11. Their father died in the wilderness so they found themselves fatherless, motherless, brotherless, husbandless, penniless and not a little hopeless. The law at that time stated that if a man died without any sons his inheritance went to his brother regardless of whether he had a daughter, as inheritance was passed from father to son and not from father to daughter. A woman was entitled to her husband's inheritance but not to her father's inheritance.

As single women, these ladies were facing complete and utter destitution. They were living on the wrong side of the law. What could they do? Surely this was the end, but somehow among the grief of losing their father and the fear for the future they stood up and decided to challenge the very law that was holding them captive. They went to Moses, the leader of Israel at that time and demanded that they be given the inheritance that they were entitled to. "'Our father died in the wilderness; but he was not in the company of those who gathered together against the Lord, in company with Korah, but he died in his own sin; and he had no sons. Why should the name of our father be removed from among his family because he had no son? Give us a possession among our father's brothers'" (Num 27:3-4 KJV). Moses took their case before the Lord and God said that these women should receive their inheritance. By standing up and refusing to settle for what life had thrown at them these women made history. After the Daughters of Zelophehad made their request the law was changed permanently so that women could receive their father's inheritance. Because these young women demanded what was theirs, generations of women following them would never be destitute.

The Daughters of Thunder fought a battle and it was a hard one but they were't the only ones to benefit from the victory that was gained. They made way for many destitute daughters coming after them. In the end their battle wasn't just about them it was about the people who came after them. I'm sure at the beginning Mahlah, Noah, Hoglah, Milcah and Tirzah wondered, "Why us? Why does life have to be so hard. We have no husband and now we have no father which leaves us with no money. If we are going to get what we deserve we have a fight on our hands. Why does this have to be our fight?" Have you ever thought that? "Why do I have to fight this battle?" Let me tell you something, in the midst of your war remember these Daughters of Thunder.

Psalm 102 says this, "When he attends to the prayer of the wretched. He won't dismiss their prayer. Write this down for the next generation so people not yet born will praise God." (Psa 102:17-18 KJV). You are not fighting just for yourself. You are fighting for the people coming after you. This fight is not just for your freedom, it is for their freedom also.

Sometimes your story will only make sense when you use it to help someone else.

Write your story so that others can glorify God after you. Your story is not for you to read or even understand. Just as my story of singleness hasn't made sense to me, I haven't always liked it or understood it, but I have written it. I have written it so that others may understand their singleness. It is my prayer that telling my story can bring healing to others.

So perhaps you understand now that you have purpose and you want to fulfill it. You want to take up your pen and write your story. But what to write? You're not prepared to settle for the blank page you've been staring at until now, you know there's a story in you but you're just not sure what it is yet.

The questions we ask bring the answers we are looking for. If that is the case then let me ask you a few that may help you write those first few sentences. Here are four questions to ask initially as you begin to write your story.

What makes you sad? When you are watching television or reading a newspaper or just walking down the street, what is it that causes those tears to come to your eyes? One minute you're fine and then the next you feel your face getting moist with the trickle that is falling down your cheek. What is it that you just saw or heard?

What makes you mad? What makes your blood boil in utter frustration? What makes you want to shout out, 'Enough is enough'? What is the one thing in the world that you want to fix?

What makes you happy? What dreams keep you awake? What do you take up in your hand that you never want to put down? What makes you want to say, 'This is why I was put on planet earth'?

What makes you feel most you? You see, purpose, calling and destiny, these are all lofty words but really they are the most natural thing in the world. Finding and fulfilling your purpose doesn't make you someone you are not, it allows you to become who you really are.

The answers to these questions are the first, small indicators of the amazing purpose that lies inside you. I remember how I used to get so frustrated at married preachers telling me how to be single. I mean, it made my blood boil!! As soon as they began to speak something in me just switched off. Everything they were saying was good and right, but I just wanted to yell, "It's okay for you! You're going back to your wonderful, cosy house and your beautiful spouse and I'm going back to an empty, lonely house with just me, myself and I for company! So don't tell me how to behave as a single person!" I would see young women just wishing their lives away as they chased after a husband. I would see them exchange the awesome purpose God had for them just so they could have a wedding ring. I would see girls who could not bear to be alone, so when they had nobody, in their search for somebody, they just settled for anybody. Do you get the picture? These things made me mad and sad. Then God challenged me. Instead of looking for a voice and being mad because there was no voice, He asked me to be that voice. He wanted me to be the answer to my own questions? He wanted me to be a solution to those problems I saw around me.

But how was I going to do that? By being happy, being me and doing those things he created me to do. What was that? Writing and speaking words of truth to whoever would listen. I am never more myself than when I am sitting at a keyboard and words come through me onto the screen. I am never more myself than when I am sharing those words with a company of people whether large or small.

What made me sad revealed what God wanted me to do and what made me happy revealed how God wanted me to do it.

Your purpose is a strange mixture of what breaks you and what makes you whole. That is a difficult balance and that is why living with purpose can be a challenge. It is like we are on the brink of what breaks our hearts and we are pulled back by fixing it with what makes us happy. Isn't God amazing? As single people if we were to focus too much on those things that break us how could we ever cope? But God has allowed us to fix those problems with what makes us. We get to do those things we love and at the same time solve the problem he has put in front of us.

We have all heard the phrase, 'outside the box.' It's a phrase that holds a lot of truth but it has been over-used to the max. I get it, we shouldn't limit ourselves, but sometimes limits are good. They are healthy and they protect us, emotionally, physically and financially. Sometimes the box we are in is exactly where God wants us to be as that is the place where we are strongest and most productive. I am a word person, they fill my box. Whether I am writing them, reading them, speaking them or listening to them, I love being surrounded by them. If I was to go 'outside the box' that I exist in and, say, work with numbers, I wouldn't survive too long. Sure, I would be 'outside the box' but I would flounder because I wouldn't be soaring with my strength. The best place for me is in my word-filled box. Paul said it right in 2 Cor 10:13 when he wrote: "We will not boast about things done outside our area of authority. We will boast only about what has happened within the boundaries of the work God has given us..."(NLT).

Maybe we don't need to live outside of the box but live inside the right one. If you feel like you are in a box right now and you cannot thrive in that environment then, by all means, get out of that box before you are suffocated, but don't just float around aimlessly - find the box thats right for you. Find a box where you can live and be the person God created you to be without hindrance. Stay there because from that box you can change the world.

Fabula Est Vestri

The one thing that motivates me in writing my story is that I don't want someone else to write the words that God has ordained for me to write. If I give up the struggle and walk away then I believe God will find someone else to finish what I started. I don't want to walk into a bookstore someday and look and see a book written by someone else that I should have written. I don't want anyone else writing my words!! I am jealous for them. God has put me on earth and kept me alive thus far so that that I should write them. Why should I give them away? Why should I let someone else write them?

Is that what you are doing? Are you throwing your words away just because it's too hard? God will wait for you as long as possible but in the end if you continue to refuse to fill the page before you He will simply ask someone else and they will write. So don't let go of your pen. Keep writing. Become jealous for your words and for the story that God has destined you to write. There is a Latin phrase, "Fabula Est Vestri," which means "the story is yours." I want you to see your purpose in this way. It is yours. No one has the right to take it from you. Whenever the enemy tempts you to walk away, declare, "this story is mine and you will not wrestle it from my hands. I may be scared and unsure of the next sentence but I will write on regardless."

You need to be this stubborn when it comes to your purpose because it is not about you. You are not the only person who will read your story. There are countless people around you and people coming after you who will read what you have written. They will read your life and it will have a direct impact on their lives.

A note about Naomi

I have spent the majority of this book speaking of Ruth and the lessons we can learn from her life, and as this book is aimed at mainly single women in their twenties and thirties this makes sense; but the more I live in this story the more I draw comfort from Naomi, the older woman in this story.

Naomi stands as a shining beacon of hope to those of us who think that our best days are over, and, believe me, you don't have to be old and decrepit to fall into that pit of despair. I am in my thirties and I have battled with that same notion that the best days of my life are behind me. I have had seasons in my life where I was riding the wave and living my dream. My days were filled with purpose and I could visibly see that purpose unfolding before my eyes, I spent my time doing what I felt I was created to do but then that season ended. Then came the season of just 'getting through the day.' Instead of living my dream it was like I was trying to survive my worst nightmare. I was no longer able to soar with the strengths I had because I was put in a situation where I struggled with my weaknesses and those glory days I revelled in a few short years ago seemed a distant memory. It was in those days that the enemy cruelly whispered in my ear, "Your best days are over. You had your opportunity. You've fulfilled your purpose and that season is over. Now just focus on surviving."

I think this is the worst lie we can hear and with it comes a sense of despair and regret. It is almost like we assume the posture of looking sadly over our shoulder grieving for what was.

In the first verse of the first chapter of the book of Ruth we see Naomi's story of how she had to leave her home because of a famine in Bethlehem. This was the place where she was born and met her husband and raised her family, then disaster struck. She had to leave everything she knew and loved. But it was okay, she still had her boys so she could endure this pain to keep them alive, a mother's love has a capacity that knows no bounds. She and her family ended up in a strange land where life would never be the same. First her husband died, then a few years later both of her sons died. Here she was in a strange land completely alone. If anyone had cause to think that her best days were over it was Naomi.

At the beginning of this story when I think of Naomi in Moab after she tragically lost her husband and two sons I can picture her looking out the window of her house in the direction of Bethlehem with a sense of longing, despair and regret. Longing to be back once again among her own people and have the freedom to worship her God; despair because it was too late and all the bridges had been burned; regret because she was the one, along with her husband, who burned those bridges when they decided to flee Bethlehem and go to Moab. Longing, despair and regret, a bitter mixture indeed.

I'm sure the words, 'if only' turned around in her mind over and over as she thought of what might have been; "If only we had stayed in Bethlehem. If only we had hung on a little while longer maybe we could have survived the famine." Of course there is no way of knowing exactly what she was thinking but we do know that she was bitter - so bitter that she decided to call herself Mara - meaning bitter (Ruth1:20).

However even in the middle of all that bitterness she found hope. Somewhere, somehow she heard that God had visited Bethlehem - her homeland - and given the people bread. Bethlehem, the House of Bread, had bread once again. With that news, hope sprang up in Naomi and she decided it was time to go home. She had spent too long in the land of pain and grief and she decided to rise up and return to her people. She returned to the people who would not reject her but welcome her back with open arms. I'm sure there were times in Moab when she wondered whether she would ever smell the bread of Bethlehem ever again but here was a small chance and she grabbed it. She would leave the trappings of Moab behind and return to her people and her God.

As she made her way back home she soon found that she had two travelling companions, Ruth and Orpah, her daughters-in-law. Naomi was quick to explain to them the pointlessness of going back to Bethlehem. She saw no future for them there. Naomi thought that her best days were behind her but she didn't believe that to be true of Ruth and Orpah - they could have happy days again if they stayed in Moab. Orpah agreed and went on her merry way back to Moab, but Ruth 'clung' to Naomi; she couldn't let her go. She pleaded with Naomi to let her to accompany her back to Bethlehem. She vowed that Naomi's people and Naomi's God would be hers. This is amazing when you consider how bitter and distraught Naomi's life was; even through all of the heartache Ruth saw something in Naomi that made her want what Naomi had. Even in Naomi's darkest hour she still shone bright and led the way home for Ruth.

So with Ruth clinging to her side she made her way back home, and with that one act she is the example that our best days are not over.

Once she arrives back in Bethlehem - her home - something re-ignited within her. She sees the potential relationship between Ruth and Boaz and she became quite the matchmaker. Instead of being defined by bitterness she let hope be born again within her.

We know that Naomi was bitter and full of despair. I'm sure that she never once thought that she would hold a grandchild in her arms, but she did. Its interesting to note that after Ruth and Boaz get married and they have their first child, the women of Bethlehem sing that, "a son has been born to Naomi" (Ruth 4:17 KJV). Not Ruth, but Naomi. Can't you hear the joy and the hope? By singing this over Naomi these women declare to all of us that our best days can still be ahead of us. Despite the pain and despite the bitterness we can hold the future in our hands just like Naomi.

Purpose does not have an an age limit.

The End

...or is it the beginning?

If you do not have a relationship with the God I have spoken so much about in this book but want to know Him then pray this simple prayer:

"Dear Jesus. Thank You for Your love that took you to the Cross to die for me. Please forgive me of my sins and come and live in my heart. Thank you that you rose from the dead and that same resurrection power is now in my life. Thank you that not only can I have a relationship with you on this earth but that I get to spend eternity with you in Heaven. Amen."

Congratulations, you have just begun the most amazing adventure of your life. Don't be shy about it, spread the news!

For me, finishing this book means that I have accomplished one of the things God asked me to do while I was on the Shelf, my time there hasn't been wasted. You are holding in your hands the very

evidence that being alone doesn't mean you are without the ability

to achieve something great and impact lives. But more important

than what you are holding in your hands is what you are holding in

your heart as a result of what you are holding in your hands. My

prayer is, as you finish this book, that you begin your own. I pray

that hope and passion are ignited inside of you and you go forward

and make the most of your time on the Shelf. Forget the shame and

put Worship, Friendship and Purpose on your Shelf and enjoy your

time together.

Acknowledgements

This book would not be possible without the help of some very special people. I want to thank Matt McGlade, Philip Sebastien Crossey, Jayne Dunlop and my mother, Rosemary McAuley for all their editorial skills.

I want to thank Christopher Havelin for his wonderful design skills in creating the book cover.

If you wish to contact the author of this book please go to www.lisajanemcauley.com or follow her on Twitter @lisajanemcauley

24788235R00076

Made in the USA
Charleston, SC
07 December 2013